Storybook *quilts*

14 QUILT DESIGNS INSPIRED BY CHILDREN'S BOOK ILLUSTRATIONS

Laura Piland

Storybook Quilts

© 2025 by Laura Piland

Special thanks to Sarah Reschke (and her kids!) for graciously sharing her home for the photography for the book.

Printed in the United States of America.

ISBN: 979-8-218-67977-4

ACKNOWLEDGMENTS

Creating this book has been a journey stitched together with love, late nights, and yards (and yards!) of fabric and thread.

To my husband—thank you for your unwavering support, constant encouragement, and belief in me, even when I was buried under piles of fabric and deadlines. You are my calm in the creative storm.

To my boys—thank you for your patience, your hugs, and perfectly-timed games of hide and seek. You remind me over and over what really matters.

To my mom—thank you for stepping in with a needle and thread (and a whole lot of love) to help me meet deadlines I wasn't sure I'd make. I couldn't have done it without you.

To my quilting colleagues—thank you for the brainstorming, collaboration, and honest conversations that helped shape this book. Your talent pushes me to grow, and your friendship makes the journey richer. I'm lucky to create alongside such generous and passionate makers.

And to the quilting community—thank you for your endless enthusiasm, kindness, and support. Your shared love of fabric and thread continues to inspire me every day. I'm so grateful to be part of a creative community that cheers each other on and celebrates every finished stitch.

This book wouldn't exist without all of you.

DEDICATION

To my three wild, wonderful boys—
Thank you for reminding me every day
that stories are meant to be shared,
books are meant to be devoured,
and laughter is the best kind of punctuation.

May you always chase adventures,
both on the page and off,
and may your shelves never run out of books
(or snacks).

Storybook *quilts*

INTRODUCTION

Once upon a time, after the chaos of the day and before bedtime, I would gather with my three boys and a pile of well-loved picture books. The stories varied—adventures with talking animals, journeys through enchanted forests, quiet tales of friendship—but no matter the story, our eyes were drawn not just to the characters or the words, but to the details in the illustrations.

"Look, Mama!" one of them would exclaim, pointing to the page. "That bear has a quilt!"
Soon, we were all quilt-spotting—patchwork blankets on beds, picnic quilts spread under trees, cozy coverlets wrapped around sleepy storybook characters. And in those small moments, I felt something begin to stir: a blend of curiosity and inspiration.

What if those quilts didn't stay on the page?

That question took root in my heart. I began stitching past their bedtime, recreating the illustrated quilts from our favorite books, bringing them to life with fabric, thread, and imagination. Each quilt became a tribute to a story we loved—a physical memory of a shared moment, a bedtime ritual, a mother and child bond.

Storybook Quilts was born from those nights. It's part quilting book, part love letter to children's literature, and wholly inspired by the magical intersection of real and make believe. Inside, you'll find quilt patterns that echo the illustrations of beloved picture books, bringing your favorite stories to life.

Whether you're an experienced quilter looking for new inspiration or a parent who treasures the quiet moments spent reading with a child, I invite you to turn the page—and begin stitching stories into memories that will last a lifetime.

Laura Piland

HOW TO USE THIS BOOK

Storybook Quilts is designed to bring stories to life—one quilt at a time, transforming story time into an experience that lasts long after the book is closed.

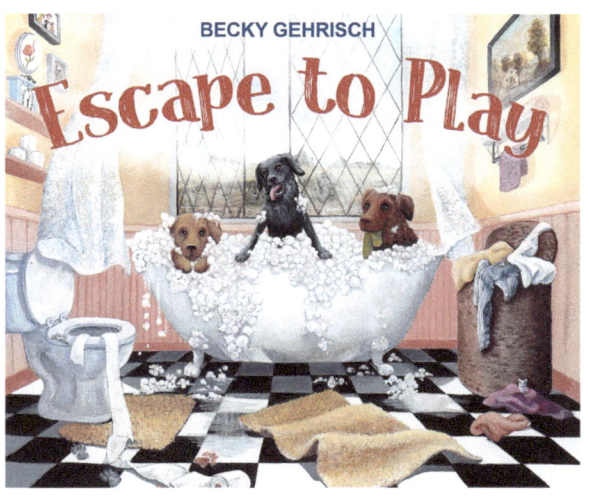

Each quilt pattern in this book is inspired by a specific children's picture book that features a quilt in its illustrations. To begin, simply choose one of the storybooks included in this book. (A complete list is on page 76.) Read the story, and look for the quilt as it appears in the illustration. Then, find the corresponding pattern in *Storybook Quilts* to recreate the quilt yourself.

As an example, the cover of the children's book *Escape to Play* by Becky Gehrisch is pictured on this page. When reading the book, you'll find the illustration shown at the right, with three mischievous dogs playing in the backyard while a quilt is hanging on the clothesline drying. In *Storybook Quilts*, the pattern for this quilt is on page 42. Fabric and color suggestions are given so you can make a quilt that closely matches the one in the pages of the picture book, bringing the story to life.

Each pattern has been thoughtfully written to reflect the look and feel of the quilt from the book illustrations. You don't need to be an expert quilter—just a lover of stories and stitching.

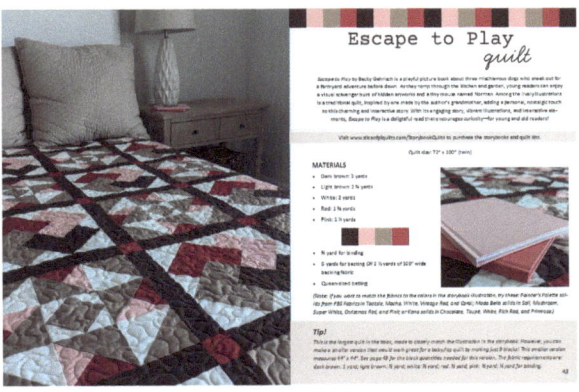

Here are just a few ways you can use the quilts in this book:

- Gift a quilt and corresponding book at a baby shower for a unique, story-inspired present.
- Make one for a grandchild, pairing it with the book for story time snuggles.
- Donate a quilt to a local library as a cozy addition to a children's reading nook.
- Offer quilts to a school or daycare for story time use or as a classroom fundraiser.
- Support a children's home or shelter with a comforting, handmade quilt and the book that inspired it.
- Create a quilt and book set to donate to a pediatric hospital or children undergoing long-term medical care.
- Give a quilt and book as a teacher gift, especially to early childhood educators or librarians.

The quilts created from the patterns in this book are more than just fabric and thread—they're warmth, comfort, imagination, and love.

Bear Can't Sleep *quilt*

The *Bear Books* series by Karma Wilson and illustrated by Jane Chapman follows the adventures of a lovable bear and his woodland friends. These stories are cherished for their rhythmic, rhyming text and heartwarming illustrations, making them ideal for bedtime reading. The books explore themes of friendship, emotions, and the changing seasons, all through the lens of Bear and his friends. In *Bear Stays Up for Christmas*, Bear receives a quilt as a gift from Santa! The patchwork quilt is featured in many other books in the series including *Bear Can't Sleep*, *Bear Feels Sick*, *Bear Says Thanks*, *Bear's Loose Tooth*, and *Bear Can't Wait*.

Visit www.sliceofpiquilts.com/StorybookQuilts to purchase the storybooks and quilt kits.

Quilt size: 32" x 40" (baby/lap)

MATERIALS

- 7 fat quarters (18" x 20")

(Note: The quilt illustration in the storybook uses seven fabrics: a navy polka dot, light blue dot, blue stripe, light blue stars, light blue solid, medium blue solid, and peach solid. You can choose similar fabrics to match the illustration, or you can be inspired by the color palette and use any blue and peach fabrics!)

- ⅓ yard for binding

- 1 yard for backing

- Crib-sized batting

Tip!

Want to make a larger quilt? Use seven half-yard cuts instead of fat quarters, then sew 14 squares in each row and make 16 rows to make a 56" x 64" quilt! This size would use ½ yard for binding and would require a package of twin-sized batting. Minky would be fun for the back! 2 yards would be perfect! (Or get 3 ¾ yards of regular quilting cotton for the back, and cut it in half and sew it together along the selvages.)

CUTTING

From *each* of the fat quarters, cut:

(12) 4 ½" x 4 ½" squares (84 total)

From the binding fabric, cut:

(4) 2 ½" x 40" strips

ASSEMBLING THE QUILT TOP

Arrange the squares into 10 rows with 8 squares in each row. (You will have 4 squares left over.) You can use the diagram on the next page as a guide, but the layout is meant to be random, so it is not necessary to copy it exactly. (Even my quilt is different than the one in the diagram!)

Sew the squares together in each row. Press the seams in odd-numbered rows to the left; press the seams in even-numbered rows to the right.

Sew the rows together, nesting seams. Press these long seams down.

Tip!

I used 80/20 batting for all the quilts in this book. This batting is 80% cotton and 20% polyester. The blend is soft and breathable, but also durable to withstand many washings. It does not require any special washing or drying instructions, so you can wash the quilt with your regular laundry. Quilts made with 80/20 batting are warm and comfortable but also practical for regular washing and use.

FINISHING THE QUILT

Layer the backing fabric (right side down), batting, and quilt top (right side up) to make a quilt sandwich. Baste and quilt as desired.

For my version, I free-motion quilted a large meander design.

Sew binding strips end to end, then bind the quilt using your favorite method. Be sure to label the quilt too!

All By Myself *quilt*

In *All By Myself*, beloved author-illustrator Mercer Mayer captures the independence and determination of childhood through the eyes of Little Critter, a fuzzy and endearing character who wants to prove he can do things on his own. From getting dressed to brushing his teeth, tying his shoes, and even helping around the house, Little Critter does many everyday tasks, proudly declaring that he can do them "all by myself"—even if he doesn't quite get everything perfect. Little Critter has a colorful patchwork quilt on his bed, and it appears in many other books in the series including *Just Go to Bed*, *I Just Forgot*, and *Just Me and My Puppy*.

Visit www.sliceofpiquilts.com/StorybookQuilts to purchase the storybooks and quilt kits.

Quilt size: 40" x 56" (baby/throw)

MATERIALS

- 6 half yards

(Note: I've used six bright solid fabrics for my quilt, but depending on the storybook that you use as inspiration, you might choose to include other colors including lavender and pink.)

- ½ yard for binding
- 1 ¾ yard for backing
- Crib-sized batting

Tip!

Try something different! Instead of the ½ yard of binding fabric, you could use the leftover pieces from the six half-yard cuts to make a scrappy binding! Just cut (2) 2 ½" x 18" strips from each color, then sew them end to end in a random order. Sew the binding to the quilt as you usually would, and it will add a playful look that makes your quilt one of a kind!

CUTTING

From *each* of the half yards, cut:

(24) 4 ½" x 4 ½" squares (144 total)

From the binding fabric, cut:

(5) 2 ½" x 40" strips

ASSEMBLING THE QUILT TOP

Arrange the squares into 14 rows with 10 squares in each row. (You will have 4 squares left over.) You can use the diagram on the next page as a guide, but the layout is meant to be random, so it is not necessary to copy it exactly. (Even my quilt is different than the one in the diagram!)

Sew the squares together in each row. Press the seams in odd-numbered rows to the left; press the seams in even-numbered rows to the right.

Sew the rows together, nesting seams. Press these long seams down.

FINISHING THE QUILT

Layer the backing fabric (right side down), batting, and quilt top (right side up) to make a quilt sandwich. Baste and quilt as desired.

For my version, I used a walking foot to stitch in the ditch of all vertical and horizontal seams. See the next page for tips on stitching in the ditch.

Sew binding strips end to end, then bind the quilt using your favorite method. Remember to add a quilt label too!

WHAT IS 'STITCH IN THE DITCH'?

One method for quilting (sewing through the quilt top, batting, and backing to hold everything together) is stitching in the ditch. This is usually done with a walking foot and means stitching right in the seam line where two pieces of fabric are joined together—or in the "ditch."

If the seams are pressed open, then the ditch is right in the middle between the two fabrics. (Figure 1)

If the seams are pressed to one side, then you stitch on the fabric that does not have the bulk of the seam with the needle as close as you can get to the other fabric. (Figure 2) Accuracy requires slow stitching, and as you can see in the top photo on the previous page, the quilting stitches are nearly hidden!

Fig. 1   Fig. 2

Chicks Run Wild *quilt*

Chicks Run Wild by Sudipta Bardhan-Quallen is an adorable, laugh-out-loud picture book that's perfect for bedtime—or maybe to read just before a bedtime *escape attempt*. In this playful tale, Mama Hen tucks her five chicks into bed—each one snuggled under a cozy brown quilt—but the moment she leaves, the wild rumpus begins—pillow fights, somersaults, and all kinds of late-night chaos! The rhyming text is bouncy and full of energy, making it engaging for little ones (and really fun to read aloud), and the illustrations by Ward Jenkins are bright, expressive, and a perfect match for the playful story.

Visit www.sliceofpiquilts.com/StorybookQuilts to purchase the storybooks and quilt kits.

Quilt size: 36" x 44" (baby/lap)

MATERIALS

- Dark brown: ½ yard
- Medium brown: 1 yard
- Light brown: ½ yard

- ½ yard for binding
- 1 ½ yards for backing
- Crib-sized batting

Tip!

When choosing solid-colored fabrics, many brands offer similar shades. Don't be afraid to mix and match across collections to get the colors you like. This can help you learn what you like—and dislike—about them too!

If you're using Painter's Palette solids from PBS Fabrics, then Golden Brown, Wheat, and Beige will work great. If you're using Moda Bella solids, then choose Sienna, Paper Bag, and Tan. Or if you're using Kona solids by Robert Kaufman, choose Earth, Wheat, and Khaki.

CUTTING

From the dark brown fabric, cut:

(30) 4 ½" x 4 ½" squares

From the medium brown fabric, cut:

(49) 4 ½" x 4 ½" squares

From the light brown fabric, cut:

(20) 4 ½" x 4 ½" squares

From the binding fabric, cut:

(5) 2 ½" x 40" strips

ASSEMBLING THE QUILT TOP

Arrange 5 dark brown squares and 4 medium brown squares to create the first row as shown in the diagram on the next page. Sew squares together. Press the seams to the left. Repeat to make 6 identical rows.

Arrange 5 medium brown squares and 4 light brown squares to create the second row as shown in the diagram on the next page. Sew squares together. Press the seams to the right. Repeat to make 5 identical rows.

Sew Row 1 and Row 2 together, then continue sewing on the additional rows, alternating row type. Nest the seams as you sew, then press the long seams down.

FINISHING THE QUILT

Layer the backing fabric (right side down), batting, and quilt top (right side up) to make a quilt sandwich. Baste and quilt as desired.

For my version, I used a walking foot to stitch about ¼" on either side of the horizontal and vertical seams.

Sew binding strips end to end, then bind the quilt using your favorite method. Be sure to include a label on the quilt too!

ALL ABOUT THREAD

I used Aurifil 50wt cotton thread to piece all the quilts in this book. This is a 2-ply, long-staple cotton thread, meaning it's strong but thinner than other brands. That feature makes it possible to wind more thread on the bobbin and have fewer bobbin changes! Another perk of Aurifil cotton thread is that it has less lint than other brands. Less lint means less time spent cleaning my sewing machine and more time sewing! For this quilt, I used a medium brown color for all the piecing, then used the same thread for the quilting too!

Llama Llama Red Pajama *quilt*

Llama Llama Red Pajama is a modern classic storybook that highlights the emotions of bedtime, especially the big feelings little ones can have when they're suddenly alone in the dark. Written and illustrated by Anna Dewdney, the book follows Baby Llama as he gets tucked in for the night, snuggled under his bright, colorful quilt in a cozy bed—but bedtime doesn't go quite as smoothly as planned. As Mama Llama heads downstairs, Baby Llama's worries begin to grow. He calls out, he waits, and his imagination runs wild. The rhyming text and expressive illustrations perfectly capture both the drama and tenderness of bedtime.

Visit www.sliceofpiquilts.com/StorybookQuilts to purchase the storybooks and quilt kits.

Quilt size: 45" x 52" (baby/throw)

MATERIALS

- 7 quarter-yard cuts of minky or fleece (about 58" wide)

(Note: I used a mix of solid fleece fabrics and dot minky fabrics for my version. This quilt would be great for using leftover pieces of minky from the backs of other quilts too!)

- ½ yard for binding
- 3 yards for backing
- Throw-sized batting (optional)

Tip!

Want to use regular quilting cotton? You can! Choose stripes, polka dots, or solid fabrics in bright colors for the same look!

You'll need 11 fat quarters. Cut the same sizes and quantities of squares, but sew with a regular ¼" seam. This will make a 48" x 56" throw size quilt. All the other fabric requirements and directions stay the same, but you'll need 6 binding strips instead of 5.

CUTTING

From *each* of the quarter yards, cut:

(24) 4 ½" x 4 ½" squares (168 total)

From the binding fabric, cut:

(5) 2 ½" x 40" strips

ASSEMBLING THE QUILT TOP

Arrange the squares into 14 rows with 12 squares in each row. You can use the diagram on the next page as a guide, but the layout is meant to be random, so it is not necessary to copy it exactly. (Even my quilt is different than the one in the diagram!)

Sew the squares together in each row using a ⅜" seam. (Yes, this is slightly larger than a typical quilting seam, but these fabrics are a bit bulkier than quilting fabrics too.)

DO NOT PRESS! Minky and fleece fabrics are polyester and can melt when pressed with a hot iron! Instead, use a wood or plastic seam roller to press the seams open.

Sew the rows together, lining up the pressed open seams. (I like to align the seams, then put one pin to hold the layers just before the seam, and another pin just after the seam. This helps the fabric from shifting as I approach the seam when sewing. Then just remove the pins when you get near them as you sew.) Use the seam roller to press the long seams open.

TIPS FOR WORKING WITH MINKY

- Minky will not fray, but it will create lots of fuzz when cutting. Use a lint roller or small portable vacuum to clean as you cut. Work outside if the weather permits!

- When using a rotary cutter to cut out the squares, use a scrap of fleece or minky to "scrub" the fuzzies off of your cutting mat. Shake the squares outside to remove any extra fuzz.

- Minky will not shrink when washed. You can prewash the cotton backing fabric before making the quilt if desired.

- Minky is polyester, and it can melt if ironed or dried with high heat! Be sure to wash the finished quilt in cold water and dry on low heat.

- Be sure to clean your sewing machine after sewing with minky!

FINISHING THE QUILT

Cut backing fabric into two equal lengths. Trim off selvages. Sew the two pieces together along the selvage edge using a ½" seam. Press this seam open.

Layer the backing fabric (right side down), batting, and quilt top (right side up) to make a quilt sandwich.

(Note: When using minky and fleece fabrics, batting is optional. I still use it in my quilts because I love the weight and texture that it adds to the quilt after quilting.)

Baste and quilt as desired.

For my version, I used a large free-motion meander design.

Sew binding strips end to end, then bind the quilt using your favorite method. Don't forget to add a label too!

The Prince's Bedtime *quilt*

In The *Prince's Bedtime*, Joanne Oppenheim spins a whimsical tale about a young prince who simply refuses to go to sleep. Despite the royal staff's best efforts—offering stories, songs, snacks, and more—the prince stays in his grand bedroom, tucked beneath his green patchwork quilt but wide awake. Nothing seems to work until a wise woman arrives with a simple, soothing solution: the perfect bedtime story. With lyrical rhymes, colorful illustrations, and gentle humor, this charming book celebrates the magic of storytelling and the power of a good book—perfect for bedtime snuggles!

Visit www.sliceofpiquilts.com/StorybookQuilts to purchase the storybooks and quilt kits.

Quilt size: 48" x 60" (lap/throw)

MATERIALS

- 12 fat quarters (18" x 20")

(Note: I've used solid green fabrics for the illustrations throughout the pattern, but the storybook illustration uses print fabrics. Raid your stash or look for green fabrics including geometric, batik, and floral designs.)

- ½ yard for binding
- 3 yards for backing
- Twin-sized batting
- 12wt cotton thread or embroidery floss for hand stitching accents (dark green and white)

Tip!

12wt cotton thread is thicker than typical machine sewing thread. It is often used for hand applique, hand embroidery, hand quilting, cross stitch, and a blanket stitch. It's similar to embroidery floss, which can be used in the same ways. When using a thicker thread, you'll want to choose a needle that has a larger eye. Embroidery needles or chenille needles are a great choice!

CUTTING

From *each* fat quarter, cut:

(1) 8 ½" x 8 ½" square (12 total)

(1) 8 ½" x 10 ½" rectangle (12 total)

(1) 8 ½" x 12 ½" rectangle (12 total)

From the binding fabric, cut:

(6) 2 ½" x 40" strips

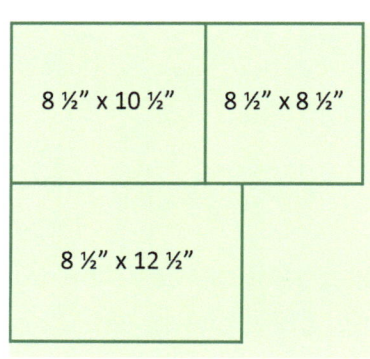

ASSEMBLING THE QUILT TOP

This quilt top is sewn in *columns* rather than rows.

Choose 2 of each size of square and rectangle, each from a different fabric. Arrange these 6 pieces into a column and sew together along the short sides. You can use the diagram on the next page as a guide, but it is not necessary to copy it exactly. Press the seams down.

Choose another 6 pieces: 2 of each size of square and rectangle from different fabrics. Arrange these pieces into a second column and sew together. Press the seams up.

Repeat to make six columns. Change the order of the pieces in each column so most of the seams do not match up between adjoining columns. Press the seams in columns 1, 3, and 5 down, and press the seams in columns 2, 4, and 6 up.

Sew the columns together. Press these long seams open or to one side.

FINISHING THE QUILT

Cut backing fabric into two equal lengths. Trim off selvages. Sew the two pieces together along the selvage edge using a ½" seam. Press this seam open.

Layer the backing fabric (right side down), batting, and quilt top (right side up) to make a quilt sandwich.

Baste and quilt as desired.

For my version, I used a medium-sized free-motion meander design.

Sew binding strips end to end, then bind the quilt using your favorite method. Add a label too!

You can call the quilt finished at this point, OR you can add hand stitching to match the illustrations in the storybook! Cut a length of 12wt cotton thread or embroidery floss, thread it through a needle, and knot the end of the thread. Choose a square or rectangle on the quilt to stitch around (or a seam to stitch along). Take the first stitch in the seam and bury the knot. Continue stitching with your desired stitch. I only stitched through the top and batting (not through to the back), but you can stitch through all the layers if you want! When finished stitching, tie a knot, trim the thread just past the knot, then bury the thread. I chose about six spots on my quilt to add this hand stitching detail: some using dark green thread, and some using white thread.

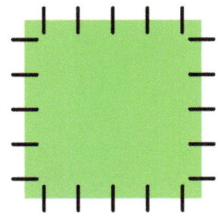

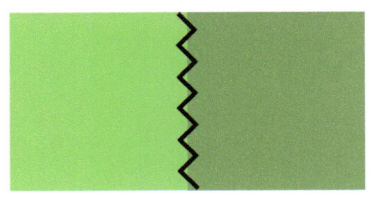

Be sure to add a label to the quilt too!

Beneath *quilt*

In *Beneath*, Cori Doerrfeld tenderly explores emotions we often keep hidden. Finn is having a hard day, and he wraps himself in a quilt to hide from the world. Grandpa invites him on a walk, and as they explore what lies beneath dirt and water, Finn uncovers the feelings buried inside him. Finn wears the quilt throughout the story, but by the end of the walk, he sees that Grandpa is carrying something too. He offers the quilt to Grandpa—realizing that comfort is something we can give, not just receive. With warm illustrations and an empathetic message, *Beneath* is a moving story about grief, love, and the healing power of being there for one another.

Visit www.sliceofpiquilts.com/StorybookQuilts to purchase the storybooks and quilt kits.

Quilt size: 54" x 54" (lap/throw)

MATERIALS

- 17 fat quarters of assorted solid colors (18" x 21")

(Note: To match the storybook illustrations, choose muted and secondary colors like pinks, corals, oranges, light blues, greens, and purples. This is a great opportunity to use solid colored scraps, and you can use more colors as long as the total is equivalent to at least 17 fat quarters.)

- 1 ¼ yards solid white for sashing
- ¼ yard pastel yellow for inner border
- 1 yard blue for outer border and binding
- 3 ½ yards for backing
- Throw-sized batting

Tip!

I used a mix of solid color brands from my scrap bins for the blocks. For the outer border and binding, try Moda Bella Sea or Kona Evening. For the inner border, try Moda Bella 30's Yellow or Kona Lemon. For the sashing, try Moda Bella Porcelain or Kona Bone.

CUTTING

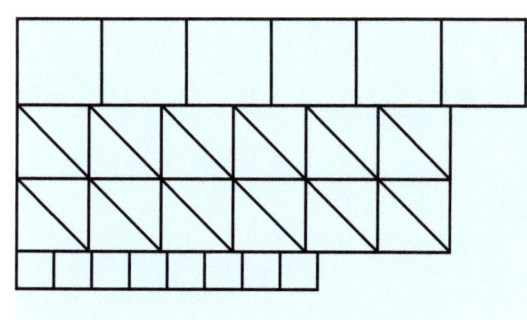

From *each* fat quarter, cut:

(6) 3 ⅜" x 3 ⅜" squares (102 total; 2 extra)

(12) 2 ⅞" x 2 ⅞" squares* (204 total; 4 extra)

(8) 1 ½" x 1 ½" squares (136 total; 15 extra)

*Subcut all 2 ⅞" x 2 ⅞" squares by cutting each square in half diagonally once to yield 400 triangles

From the white sashing fabric, cut:

(28) 1 ½" x WOF (width of fabric) strips, then subcut into

(220) 1 ½" x 4 ½" rectangles

From the yellow inner border fabric, cut:

(4) 1" x 40" strips

(2) 1" x 12" strips

(2) 1" x 13" strips

From the blue outer border/binding fabric, cut:

(4) 1 ½" x 40" strips

(2) 1 ½" x 13" strips

(2) 1 ½" x 15" strips

(6) 2 ½" x 40" strips (for binding)

SEWING THE BLOCKS

Choose one 3 ⅜" x 3 ⅜" square of one color and (4) triangles of another color.

Lightly press the square in half both horizontally and vertically to create crease lines.

Center one triangle on one side of the square right sides together and sew with a scant ¼" seam. Repeat on the opposite side of the square. Press seams towards the triangles. Trim off the points of the triangles to be even with the sides of the square.

SEWING THE BLOCKS, CONTINUED

Center one triangle on one of the remaining sides of the square, right sides together, and sew with a scant ¼" seam. Repeat on the opposite side of the square. Press seams towards the triangles.

Trim to 4 ½" square. Ideally, this should be ¼" beyond each of the square points.

*If the points of the center square are less than ¼" away from the edge of the trimmed block, then try sewing the next block with a very slightly larger seam allowance.

*If the points of the center square are more than ¼" away from the edge of the trimmed block, then try sewing the next block with a very slightly smaller seam allowance.

** Don't worry if your blocks aren't perfect! Many of mine aren't perfect either! Aim for 4 ½" x 4 ½" trimmed blocks more than making perfect seams.

Repeat all steps to make 100 blocks.

ASSEMBLING THE QUILT TOP

Using the diagram on the next page as a guide, arrange the blocks into 10 rows with 10 blocks in each row. Place a 1 ½" x 4 ½" white rectangle as a sashing strip between all the blocks. Place the 1 ½" x 1 ½" squares as cornerstones between the sashing strips.

Row 1 is only cornerstones and sashing strips. Sew these together and press seams towards the sashing pieces.

Row 2 is sashing strips and blocks. Sew these together and press seams towards the sashing strips.

Continue sewing all rows, pressing the seams the same as in rows 1 and 2.

Sew the rows together, nesting seams. Press the long seams towards the sashing rows.

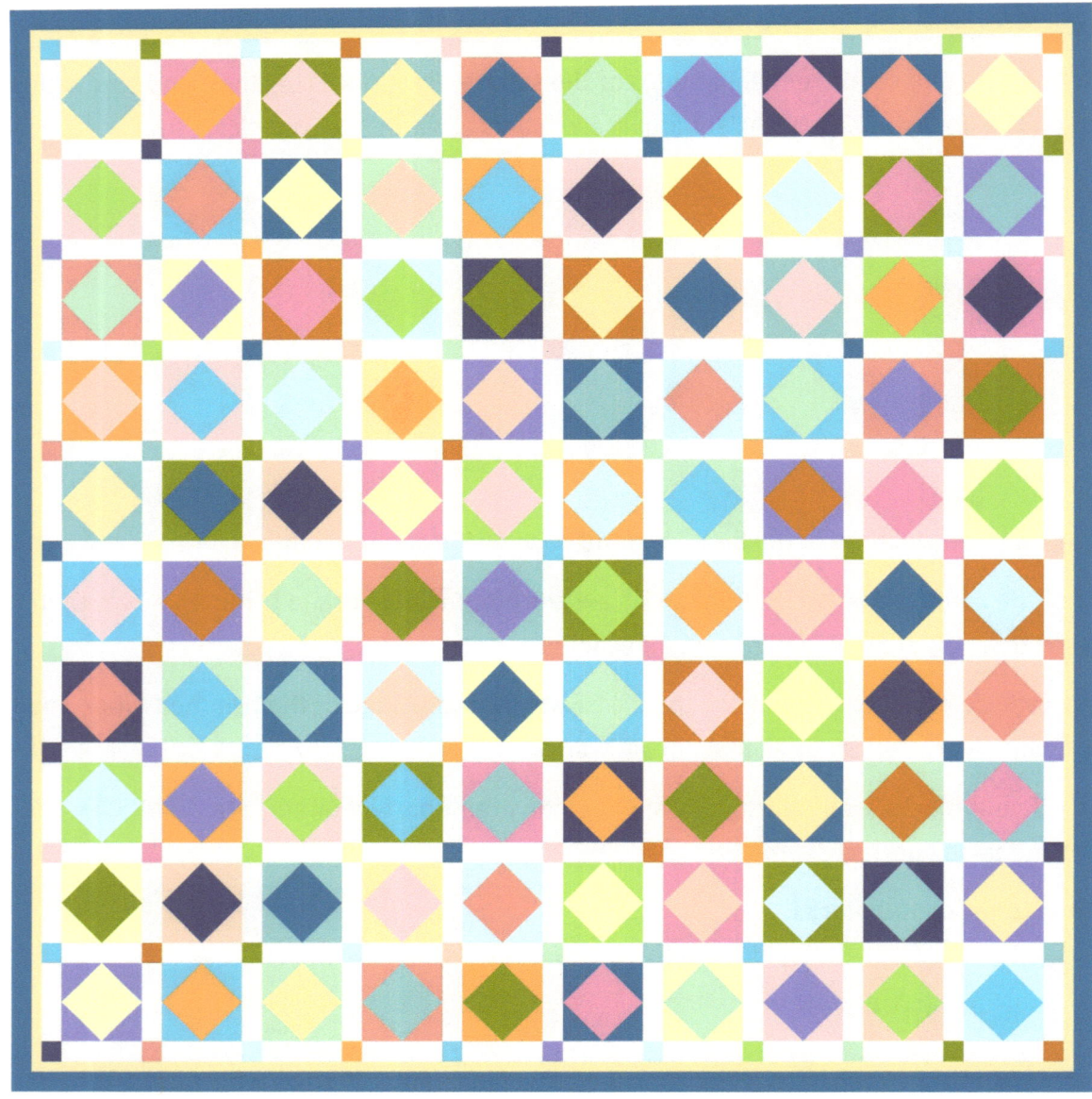

ADDING THE BORDERS

Sew a 1" x 40" yellow strip and a 1" x 12" yellow strip end to end. Press seam as desired. Pin this strip right sides together to the right side of the quilt top, pinning first the middle then the ends. (See the "tip" on the next page.) Sew and press seam towards the border fabric. Repeat for the left side.

Sew a 1" x 40" yellow strip and a 1" x 13" yellow strip end to end. Press seam as desired. Pin this strip right sides together to the top edge of the quilt top, pinning first the middle then the ends. (See the "tip" on the next page.) Sew and press seam towards the border fabric. Repeat for the bottom edge.

Sew a 1 ½" x 40" blue strip and a 1 ½" x 13" blue strip end to end. Press seam as desired. Pin this strip right sides together to the right side of the quilt top, pinning first the middle then the ends. (See the "tip" on the next page.) Sew and press seam towards the outer border. Repeat for the left side.

Sew a 1 ½" x 40" blue strip and a 1 ½" x 15" blue strip end to end. Press seam as desired. Pin this strip right sides together to the top edge of the quilt top, pinning first the middle then the ends. (See the "tip" on the next page.) Sew and press seam towards the border fabric. Repeat for the bottom edge.

FINISHING THE QUILT

Cut backing fabric into two equal lengths. Trim off selvages. Sew the two pieces together along the selvage edge using a ½" seam. Press this seam open.

Layer the backing fabric (right side down), batting, and quilt top (right side up) to make a quilt sandwich.

Baste and quilt as desired.

For my version, I used my walking foot to stitch about ¼" away from the sashing seams. This put two lines of stitching on the sashing, creating a neat design in the cornerstones where the stitching lines overlapped.

Sew binding strips end to end, then bind the quilt using your favorite method.

Remember to add a label to the quilt too!

TIPS FOR SEWING BORDERS

When adding the borders to the quilt top, pins are your friend! Fold the border strip in half and lightly finger press to mark the center. Do the same to the quilt top. Align the center marks and pin. Next, pin both ends of the border strip to the quilt top corners. Continue adding pins about every 5". If the border fabric and quilt top seem to be different lengths, try to even out the excess fabric between as many pins as you can between the corner and middle points. Whichever side (border fabric or quilt top) seems to have more fullness or excess fabric, place that side towards the feed dogs of your sewing machine. The feed dogs will help ease in the extra fabric as you sew. If the border and quilt top measurements seem too far off to work well without large puckers, then measure your quilt top and cut your borders to match that measurement before sewing. You may also want to check the accuracy of your ¼" seam for future projects.

Little Witch Hazel *quilt*

Little Witch Hazel by Phoebe Wall is a whimsical collection of four seasonal stories following a small forest witch named Hazel. She's not your typical witch—she's a caregiver, a helper, and a steadfast friend to the animals of the forest. Whether she's lending a helping hand to a neighbor or simply enjoying the peace of the forest, Hazel is guided by kindness and quiet purpose. At home in her cozy stump house, a handmade quilt rests on her bed, a symbol of the warmth and comfort she brings to others. With rich illustrations and a deep appreciation for nature, this book is a celebration of community, caretaking, and the beauty of small things.

Visit www.sliceofpiquilts.com/StorybookQuilts to purchase the storybooks and quilt kits.

Quilt size: 42" x 54" (lap/throw)

MATERIALS

- Red: 1 ¼ yards

- Blue polka dot: 1 ¼ yards

- White: 1 yard for border and binding

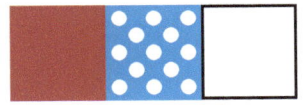

- 2 ¾ yards for backing

- Throw-sized batting

- Black cotton or acrylic yarn

- Chenille needle with a large eye

Tip!

Because this quilt has white fabric for the borders, a bleached cotton, bleached 80/20, or polyester batting would work best. This will help the white fabric to still look white after quilting. Using a natural cotton batting that's a cream or tan color will wash out the white and make it look dingy. Natural cotton batting often has flecks of brown pieces leftover from the cotton plants that can also show through white and light colored fabrics.

CUTTING

From the red fabric, cut:

(24) 7" x 7" squares

From the blue polka dot fabric, cut:

(24) 7" x 7" squares

From the white fabric, cut:

(2) 3 ½" x 36 ½" strips

(2) 3 ½" x 40" strips

(2) 3 ½" x 15" strips

(5) 2 ½" x 40" strips (for binding)

SEWING THE BLOCKS

Use a fabric marking pen/pencil to draw a diagonal line on the back of all red squares. Place one red square right sides together with a blue polka dot square. Sew ¼" on either side of the drawn line. Cut apart on the drawn line and press seam to one side to make two half square triangles (HSTs). Trim to 6 ½" square. Repeat with all red and blue polka dot squares to make 48 HSTs.

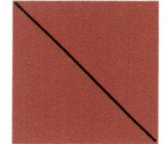 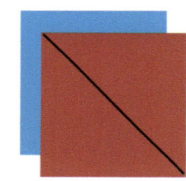 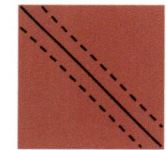 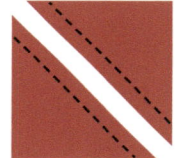  

ASSEMBLING THE QUILT TOP

Arrange the blocks into 8 rows with 6 blocks in each row. Be sure to place the blocks all facing the same direction. Use the diagram on the next page as a guide.

Sew the blocks together in each row. Press the seams in odd-numbered rows to the left; press the seams in even-numbered rows to the right.

Sew the rows together, nesting seams. Press these long seams down.

ADDING THE BORDERS

Sew a 3 ½" x 36 ½" white strip to the top edge of the quilt top. (See the "tip" on page 33.) Press seam towards the border fabric. Repeat for the bottom edge.

Sew a 3 ½" x 40" white strip and a 3 ½" x 15" white strip end to end. Press seam as desired. Sew this strip to the left side of the quilt top. (See the "tip" on page 33.) Press seam towards the border fabric. Repeat for the right side.

FINISHING THE QUILT

This quilt is tied instead of being machine quilted. There are a couple methods for doing this, but these are the steps for how I finished mine.

Cut backing fabric into two equal lengths. Trim off selvages. Sew the two pieces together along the selvage edge using a ½" seam. Press this seam open.

Layer the backing fabric (right side down), batting, and quilt top (right side up) to make a quilt sandwich.

Baste as desired, ensuring the border edges are basted well. I used curved safety pins to baste, and I put extra near the edges of the quilt top along the border edge. Trim away excess batting and backing fabric.

Sew binding strips end to end, then bind the quilt using your favorite method.

Cut a length of yarn and thread it through the eye of the chenille needle. From the front of the quilt, insert the needle about ⅛" away from the center seam of one block. Be sure the needle goes through all the layers including the backing fabric, then bring the needle back up on the other side of the seam, about ⅛" away from the seam. Pull the yarn through and leave about a 3" tail. Cut the yarn to leave another 3" tail. Tie the two tails of yarn together using a square knot (or "double knot" in shoe-tying terms). Trim both tails to be about 1" long. Repeat for all blocks. If desired, add a drop of seam sealant or fabric glue to each knot to help keep them from coming undone over time.

Be sure to add a label to the quilt too!

Miss Rumphius *quilt*

Miss Rumphius by Barbara Cooney is a timeless picture book about Alice, who sets out to live a life filled with adventure, beauty, and purpose. Miss Rumphius—as she becomes known—fulfills her dreams and ultimately spreads beauty by planting lupine flowers all over the countryside. In her cozy seaside home, a quilt in soft lupine-inspired colors rests on her bed, echoing the flowers she loves and the life she's so thoughtfully sown. Told with quiet grace and beautiful illustrations, the story encourages readers to seek wonder, live with purpose, and leave the world better than they found it.

Visit www.sliceofpiquilts.com/StorybookQuilts to purchase the storybooks and quilt kits.

Quilt size: 54" x 66" (throw)

MATERIALS

- Light blue: 1 ¼ yards

- Medium blue: 1 ¾ yards (includes binding)

- White: 1 ¾ yards

- 3 ½ yards for backing

- Twin-sized batting

CUTTING

From the light blue fabric, cut:

(25) 7 ½" x 7 ½" squares

From the medium blue fabric, cut:

(25) 7 ½" x 7 ½" squares

(7) 2 ½" x 40" strips (for binding)

From the white fabric, cut:

(49) 6 ½" x 6 ½" squares

Tip!

If you're trying to match the colors in the storybook illustration, try Painter's Palette solids by PBS Fabrics in Baby Blue and Daydream, or Moda Bella solids in Surf and 30's Blue, or Kona solid fabrics in Lake and Periwinkle.

SEWING THE BLOCKS

Use a fabric marking pen/pencil to draw a diagonal line on the back of all light blue squares. Place one light blue square right sides together with a medium blue square. Sew ¼" on either side of the drawn line. Cut apart on the drawn line and press seam to the darker fabric to make two half-square triangles (HSTs). Repeat with all light blue and medium blue fabrics to make 50 HSTs.

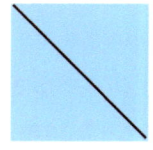 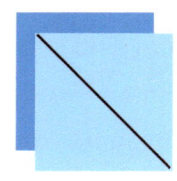 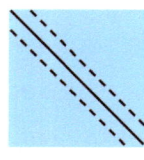 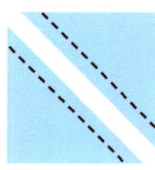  

Draw a diagonal line on the back of one HST in the opposite direction of the seam. Place this HST right sides together with another HST with the diagonal seams going in the same direction and the colored triangles on opposite sides. (Medium blue on top of light blue, and light blue on top of medium blue.) Nest the seam. Sew ¼" on either side of the drawn line. Cut apart on the drawn line. Press seam open. Trim to 6 ½" square. Repeat to make 50 quarter-square triangle (QST) blocks.

  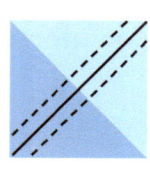 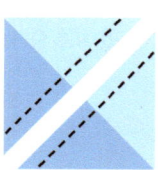  

ASSEMBLING THE QUILT TOP

Arrange the blocks and white squares into 11 rows with 9 total blocks and squares in each row. Use the diagram on the next page as a guide, paying attention to the orientation of each block.

Sew the blocks and squares together in each row. Press the seams toward the white squares.

Sew the rows together, nesting seams. Press these long seams as desired.

FINISHING THE QUILT

Cut backing fabric into two equal lengths. Trim off selvages. Sew the two pieces together along the selvage edge using a ½" seam. Press this seam open.

Layer the backing fabric (right side down), batting, and quilt top (right side up) to make a quilt sandwich. Baste and quilt as desired.

For my version, I used my walking foot to stitch in the ditch along the seams of the QST blocks. (See page 15 for more information about stitching in the ditch.)

Sew binding strips end to end, then bind the quilt using your favorite method. Don't forget to add a label!

Escape to Play *quilt*

Escape to Play by Becky Gehrisch is a playful picture book about three mischievous dogs who sneak out for a farmyard adventure before dawn. As they romp through the kitchen and garden, young readers can enjoy a visual scavenger hunt of hidden artworks and a tiny mouse named Norman. Among the lively illustrations is a traditional quilt, inspired by one made by the author's grandmother, adding a personal, nostalgic touch to this charming and interactive story. With its engaging story, vibrant illustrations, and interactive elements, *Escape to Play* is a delightful read that encourages curiosity—for young and old readers!

Visit www.sliceofpiquilts.com/StorybookQuilts to purchase the storybooks and quilt kits.

Quilt size: 72" x 100" (twin)

MATERIALS

- Dark brown: 3 yards

- Light brown: 2 ⅜ yards

- White: 2 yards

- Red: 1 ⅜ yards

- Pink: 1 ¼ yards

- ¾ yard for binding

- 6 yards for backing *OR* 2 ½ yards of 108" wide backing fabric

- Queen-sized batting

(Note: If you want to match the fabrics to the colors in the storybook illustration, try these: Painter's Palette solids from PBS Fabrics in Tootsie, Mocha, White, Vintage Red, and Coral; Moda Bella solids in Soil, Mushroom, Super White, Christmas Red, and Pink; or Kona solids in Chocolate, Taupe, White, Rich Red, and Primrose.)

Tip!

This is the largest quilt in the book, made to closely match the illustration in the storybook. However, you can make a smaller version that would work great for a baby/lap quilt by making just 9 blocks! This smaller version measures 44" x 44". See page 49 for the block quantities needed for this version. The fabric requirements are: dark brown: 1 yard; light brown: ½ yard; white: ⅔ yard; red: ⅓ yard; pink: ⅓ yard; ½ yard for binding.

CUTTING

From the dark brown fabric, cut:

(2) 5 ½" x WOF (width of fabric) strips, then subcut into:

    (9) 5 ½" x 5 ½" squares, cut in half diagonally *twice* to yield (36) A triangles

(3) 5" x WOF strips, then subcut into:

    (18) 5" x 5" squares

(29) 2 ½" x WOF strips, then subcut into:

    (58) 2 ½" x 12 ½" rectangles

    (6) 2 ½" x 40" rectangles

    (2) 2 ½" x 33" rectangles

    (2) 2 ½" x 17 ½" rectangles

From the light brown fabric, cut:

(2) 5 ½" x WOF strips, then subcut into:

    (9) 5 ½" x 5 ½" squares, cut in half diagonally *twice* to yield (36) A triangles

(12) 5" x WOF strips, then subcut into:

    (86) 5" x 5" squares

(2) 3 ⅜" x WOF strips, then subcut into:

    (17) 3 ⅜" x 3 ⅜" squares

From the white fabric, cut:

(3) 5 ½" x WOF strips, then subcut into:

    (18) 5 ½" x 5 ½" squares, cut in half diagonally *twice* to yield (72) A triangles

(9) 5" x WOF strips, then subcut into:

    (70) 5" x 5" squares

(3) 2 ⅞" x WOF strips, then subcut into:

    (34) 2 ⅞" x 2 ⅞" squares, cut in half diagonally *once* to yield (68) B triangles

CUTTING, CONTINUED

From the red fabric, cut:

(4) 5 ½" x WOF strips, then subcut into:

    (26) 5 ½" x 5 ½" squares, cut in half diagonally *twice* to yield (104) A triangles

(3) 5" x WOF strips, then subcut into:

    (18) 5" x 5" squares

(2) 2 ½" x WOF strips, then subcut into:

    (24) 2 ½" x 2 ½" squares

From the pink fabric, cut:

(4) 5 ½" x WOF strips, then subcut into:

    (26) 5 ½" x 5 ½" squares, cut in half diagonally *twice* to yield (104) A triangles

(3) 5" x WOF strips, then subcut into:

    (18) 5" x 5" squares

From the binding fabric, cut:

(9) 2 ½" x 40" strips

SEWING THE BLOCKS

This quilt is made with two different quilt blocks. The blocks are made up of smaller blocks or units. Some of these units are used in both blocks. For this pattern, all similar units are made at the same time, regardless of which block they will create in the end. I recommend sewing all of one type of unit before moving to the next.

First, let's make half-square triangles (HST).

Use a fabric marking pen/pencil to draw a diagonal line on the back of all white 5" squares.

Place one white 5" square right sides together with a red 5" square. Sew ¼" on either side of the drawn line. Cut apart on the drawn line and press seam to the red fabric to make 2 white/red half-square triangles (HSTs). Trim to 4 ½" square.

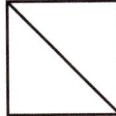 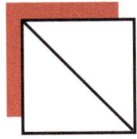  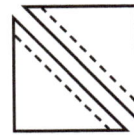  

Repeat with other 5" squares to make the following HST color combinations and quantities. (Note: This will not use all of the 5" squares of each color, as those will be used in a later step.)

      Make 18   Make 18   Make 18   Make 86

SEWING THE BLOCKS, CONTINUED

Next, let's make split quarter-square triangles (QST).

Cut a red 5" square in half diagonally *once* to yield (2) C triangles.

Arrange a red C triangle, a white A triangle, and a pink A triangle as shown. Sew the white and pink triangles together first along their short sides. Press towards the pink triangle. Sew this pink/white triangle to the red C triangle to make the red/white/pink split QST. Press the seam towards the red triangle. Trim to 4 ½" square.

Repeat with other 5" squares and A triangles to make the following split quarter-square triangle color combinations and quantities.

 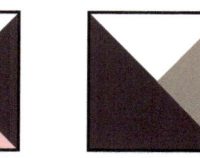  

| Make 18 | Make 18 | Make 18 | Make 18 | Make 68 |

Next is making quarter-square triangle (QST) blocks.

Arrange a red, pink, dark brown, and light brown A triangle as shown. Sew the red and pink triangles together first along their short sides. Press the seam towards the red fabric. Then sew the dark brown and light brown triangles together along their short sides. Press the seam towards the dark brown fabric. Sew the two triangle pairs together, nesting the center seam. Press seam open. Trim to 4 ½" square. Repeat to make 18 QST blocks.

Make 18

The last type of unit to sew is a square in a square unit.

Lightly press a light brown 3 ⅜" square in half both horizontally and vertically to create crease lines.

Center one white B triangle on one side of the square right sides together and sew with a scant ¼" seam. Repeat on the opposite side of the square. Press seams towards the triangles. Trim off the points of the triangles to be even with the sides of the square.

  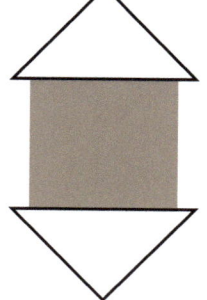 

SEWING THE BLOCKS, CONTINUED

Center one triangle on one of the remaining sides of the square, right sides together, and sew with a scant ¼" seam. Repeat on the opposite side of the square. Press seams towards the triangles.

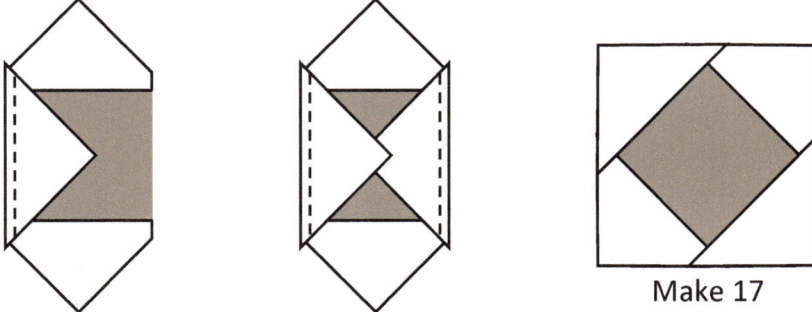

Make 17

Trim to 4 ½" square. Ideally, this should be ¼" beyond each of the square points.

*If the points of the center square are less than ¼" away from the edge of the trimmed block, then try sewing the next block with a very slightly larger seam allowance.

*If the points of the center square are more than ¼" away from the edge of the trimmed block, then try sewing the next block with a very slightly smaller seam allowance.

** Don't worry if your blocks aren't perfect! Many of mine aren't perfect either! Aim for 4 ½" x 4 ½" trimmed blocks more than making perfect seams.

Repeat all steps to make 17 square in a square blocks.

Now it's time to assemble the quilt blocks from these units!

Using the diagrams as a guide, arrange nine units as shown, paying special attention to the orientation of each unit. Sew the three units in the top row together, and press the seams to the left. Sew the units in the middle row together, pressing these seams to the right. Sew the units in the bottom row together, pressing the seams to the left. Sew all rows together, nesting seams. Press these seams as desired. Repeat to make 18 card trick blocks and 17 star blocks.

Make 18

Make 17

47

ASSEMBLING THE QUILT TOP

Arrange the blocks into 7 rows with 5 blocks in each row. Be sure to place the blocks all facing the same direction. Use the diagram below as a guide.

Place a dark brown 2 ½" x 12 ½" rectangle as a sashing strip between all the blocks. Place the red 2 ½" x 2 ½" squares as cornerstones between the sashing strips.

Sew the blocks together in each row. Row 1 is blocks and sashing strips. Row 2 is sashing strips and cornerstones. Press the seams toward the sashing strips.

Sew the rows together, nesting seams. Press these long seams toward the sashing rows.

ADDING THE BORDERS

Sew (2) 2 ½" x 40" dark brown strips and (1) 2 ½" x 17 ½" dark brown strip end to end. Press seams as desired. Sew this strip to the left side of the quilt top. (See the "tip" on page 33.) Press seam towards the border fabric. Repeat for the right side.

Sew (1) 2 ½" x 40" dark brown strip and (1) 2 ½" x 33" dark brown strip end to end. Press seam as desired. Sew this strip to the top edge of the quilt top. (See the "tip" on page 33.) Press seam towards the border fabric. Repeat for the bottom edge.

FINISHING THE QUILT

Cut backing fabric into two equal lengths. Trim off selvages. Sew the two pieces together along the selvage edge using a ½" seam. Press this seam open.

Layer the backing fabric (right side down), batting, and quilt top (right side up) to make a quilt sandwich. Baste and quilt as desired.

For my version, I used a medium-sized free-motion meander design.

Sew binding strips end to end, then bind the quilt using your favorite method. Make sure you add a label to the quilt as well!

MAKE IT SMALLER

If you don't want to make the large twin-sized quilt, then make this smaller baby/lap size quilt! The fabric requirements are listed on page 43. All the cutting sizes and directions stay the same, but you only make 5 card trick blocks and 4 star blocks.

The quantities needed of each unit are below. This version uses (12) 2 ½" x 12 ½" sashing strips and (4) 2 ½" x 2 ½" cornerstone squares. For the borders, use (2) 2 ½" x 40 ½" strips on two sides, and (2) 2 ½" x 44 ½" strips on the other two sides. This version would need (5) 2 ½" x 40" strips for the binding.

Make 5   Make 5   Make 5   Make 21

Make 5   Make 5   Make 5   Make 5   Make 16

Make 5   Make 4

Can a Skeleton Have an X-ray? *quilt*

Can a Skeleton Have an X-ray? by Kyle Hughes-Odgers is the kind of book that encourages kids to see the world in new and unexpected ways. It's a whimsical picture book that invites young readers to explore a series of playful and thought-provoking questions, such as "How does sound taste?" and "Do colors smell?" A quilt made of different sized triangles can even be spotted in one of the quirky, detailed illustrations! With its engaging questions and delightful artwork, the book sparks curiosity and imagination in young readers, making it a joyful and memorable addition to any child's bookshelf.

Visit www.sliceofpiquilts.com/StorybookQuilts to purchase the storybooks and quilt kits.

Quilt size: 56" x 56" (throw)

MATERIALS

- Green solid: 2 yards
- Green stripe: 1 ¾ yards
- Green crosshatch: 1 ½ yards

- ½ yard for binding
- 3 ¼ yards for backing
- Throw-sized batting

Tip!

If you don't want to purchase a quilt kit or yardage of the stripe and crosshatch fabrics, then try something new!

Use fabric paint or markers to create your own striped and crosshatched fabric from a solid green fabric!

Painter's Palette solid fabric in Eucalyptus, Moda Bella in Circa Celadon, or Kona solid fabric in Celadon would all work well!

CUTTING

From the solid green fabric, cut:

(7) 9" x WOF (width of fabric) strips, then subcut into:

(10) 9" x 9" squares

(8) 9" x 18" rectangles

From the green stripe fabric, cut:

(4) 9" x WOF strips, then subcut into:

(6) 9" x 9" squares

(4) 9" x 18" rectangles (the stripe should run along the 9" side)

From the green crosshatch fabric, cut:

(3) 9" x WOF strips, then subcut into:

(4) 9" x 9" squares

(4) 9" x 18" rectangles

From the binding fabric, cut

(6) 2 ½" x 40" strips (for binding)

SEWING THE BLOCKS

Use a fabric marking pen/pencil to draw a diagonal line on the back of all solid green 9" squares. Place one solid green square right sides together with a green stripe square. Be sure that the stripes are vertical, and the diagonal line goes from the **top left to the bottom right**. Sew ¼" on either side of the drawn line. Cut apart on the drawn line and press seam to one side to make two half square triangles (HSTs). Trim to 8 ½" square. Repeat to make a total of 4 HSTs.

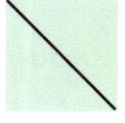 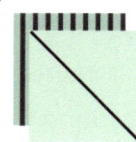 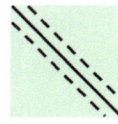  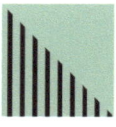 

Place one solid green square right sides together with a green stripe square. Be sure that the stripes are vertical, and the diagonal line goes from the **top right to the bottom left**. Sew ¼" on either side of the drawn line. Cut apart on the drawn line and press seam to one side to make two half square triangles (HSTs). Trim to 8 ½" square. Repeat to make a total of 8 HSTs.

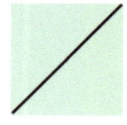 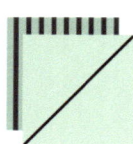 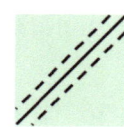 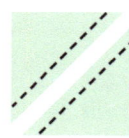 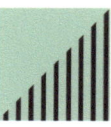 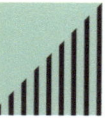

Place one solid green square right sides together with a green crosshatch square. Sew ¼" on either side of the drawn line. Cut apart on the drawn line and press seam to one side to make two half square triangles (HSTs). Trim to 8 ½" square. Repeat to make a total of 8 HSTs.

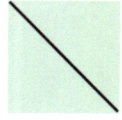  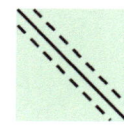   

With right sides facing up, cut (3) solid green rectangles, (1) stripe rectangle, and (2) crosshatch rectangles diagonally from the top left to the bottom right.

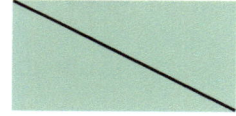 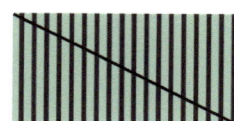 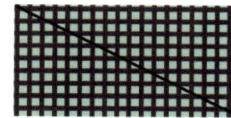

Pair a solid green triangle with a stripe or crosshatch triangle. Place right sides together, offset the points about ¼", and sew along the long side. (See the "tip" on the next page.) Press seam as desired. Trim to 8 ½" x 16 ½".

With right sides facing up, cut (5) solid green rectangles, (3) stripe rectangles, and (2) crosshatch rectangles diagonally from the top right to the bottom left.

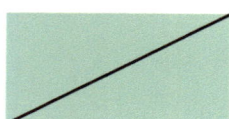  

Pair a solid green triangle with a stripe or crosshatch triangle. Place right sides together, offset the points about ¼", and sew along the long side. (See the "tip" on the next page.) Press seam as desired. Trim to 8 ½" x 16 ½".

ASSEMBLING THE QUILT TOP

Use the diagram as a guide to arrange the blocks into 7 rows. The odd-numbered rows are only made with striped blocks; the even-numbered rows are only made with crosshatch blocks.

Once laid out, sew the blocks together in each row. Press the seams in odd-numbered rows to the left; press the seams in even-numbered rows to the right.

Sew the rows together. Press these long seams as desired.

FINISHING THE QUILT

Cut backing fabric into two equal lengths. Trim off selvages. Sew the two pieces together along the selvage edge using a ½" seam. Press this seam open.

Layer the backing fabric (right side down), batting, and quilt top (right side up) to make a quilt sandwich. Baste and quilt as desired.

For my version, I quilted horizontal straight lines about 1" apart. This could be done on a longarm or with a walking foot on a regular sewing machine. (I did it with my walking foot!)

Sew binding strips end to end, then bind the quilt using your favorite method. Remember to add a label too!

TIPS FOR SEWING HALF RECTANGLE TRIANGLES

When sewing the triangles together, offset the points as shown below. The arrow indicates the "intersection" where the two triangles meet at the edge, which should be exactly where your needle sews for a ¼" seam.

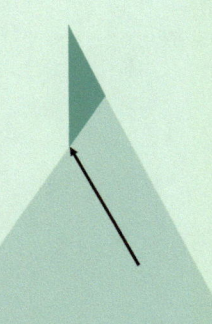

To trim the rectangles after sewing, you'll need a ruler larger than the rectangle. I butted two rulers against each other and taped them together since I don't own a large enough ruler. It's also important to note that when trimming rectangles, the seam does not meet the corner! The seam should meet ¼" in from both sides, where the seams will be after sewing. For these rectangles, use a marker to put a dot on your ruler at the ¼" x ¼" intersection and also at the 8 ¼" x 16 ¼" intersection. Align the diagonal seam with these marks, then trim to size. You'll need to flip your ruler over or put the dots at a different corner to trim the second set of rectangles where the seam goes the other direction.

Clifford *quilt*

Clifford the Small Red Puppy by Norman Bridwell is a classic children's book that tells the origin story of one of the most beloved dogs in children's literature. Emily Elizabeth remembers when Clifford was just a tiny red puppy. One night, she tucks Clifford in to bed under a colorful hexagon quilt, and the next morning he looks a bit bigger. Clifford continues to grow—and grow—into the giant red dog readers know today. The sweet story celebrates the bond between a girl and her puppy, and shows how love can help something small become something truly extraordinary.

Visit www.sliceofpiquilts.com/StorybookQuilts to purchase the storybooks and quilt kits.

Quilt size: 59" x 68" (throw)

MATERIALS

- Blue: 1 yard
- Pink: 1 yard
- Yellow: 1 yard
- Light Orange: 1 yard
- Dark Orange: ¼ yard
- Green stripe: 1 yard
- Purple heart: 1 yard
- ½ yard for binding
- 3 ½ yards for backing
- Twin-sized batting

(Note: You could use solid fabrics in aqua and violet in lieu of the print fabrics and use fabric paint or permanent fabric markers to add your own hearts and stripes!)

Tip!

Choose your favorite brand of solid fabrics to make your quilt! Here are the colors I would choose if using the following brands. Painter's Palette solids: Bright Aqua, Bubblegum, Bright Yellow, Apricot, and Fireworks; Moda Bella solids: Bright Turquoise, Fuchsia, Sunflower, Melon, and Geranium; Kona solids: Peacock, Azalea, Canary, Mango, and Coral.

CUTTING

Trace the half hexagon template from the next page onto template plastic (or make a photocopy of the template onto cardstock) and cut out. Trace the half hexagon shape onto the blue, pink, yellow, green stripe, and purple heart fabrics to get the quantities listed below then cut them out.

From the blue fabric, cut:

(7) 4 ½" x WOF (width of fabric) strips, then subcut into 27 half hexagons

From the pink fabric, cut:

(7) 4 ½" x WOF strips, then subcut into 26 half hexagons

From the yellow fabric, cut:

(7) 4 ½" x WOF strips, then subcut into 28 half hexagons

From the green stripe fabric, cut:

(6) 4 ½" x WOF strips, then subcut into 24 half hexagons

From the purple heart fabric, cut:

(6) 4 ½" x WOF strips, then subcut into 24 half hexagons

From the light orange fabric, cut:

(12) 2 ⅜" x WOF strips

From the dark orange fabric, cut:

(6) ¾" x WOF strips

From the binding fabric, cut:

(7) 2 ½" x 40" strips

Trace the triangle template from the next page onto template plastic (or make a photocopy of the template onto cardstock) and cut out to use when sewing the blocks.

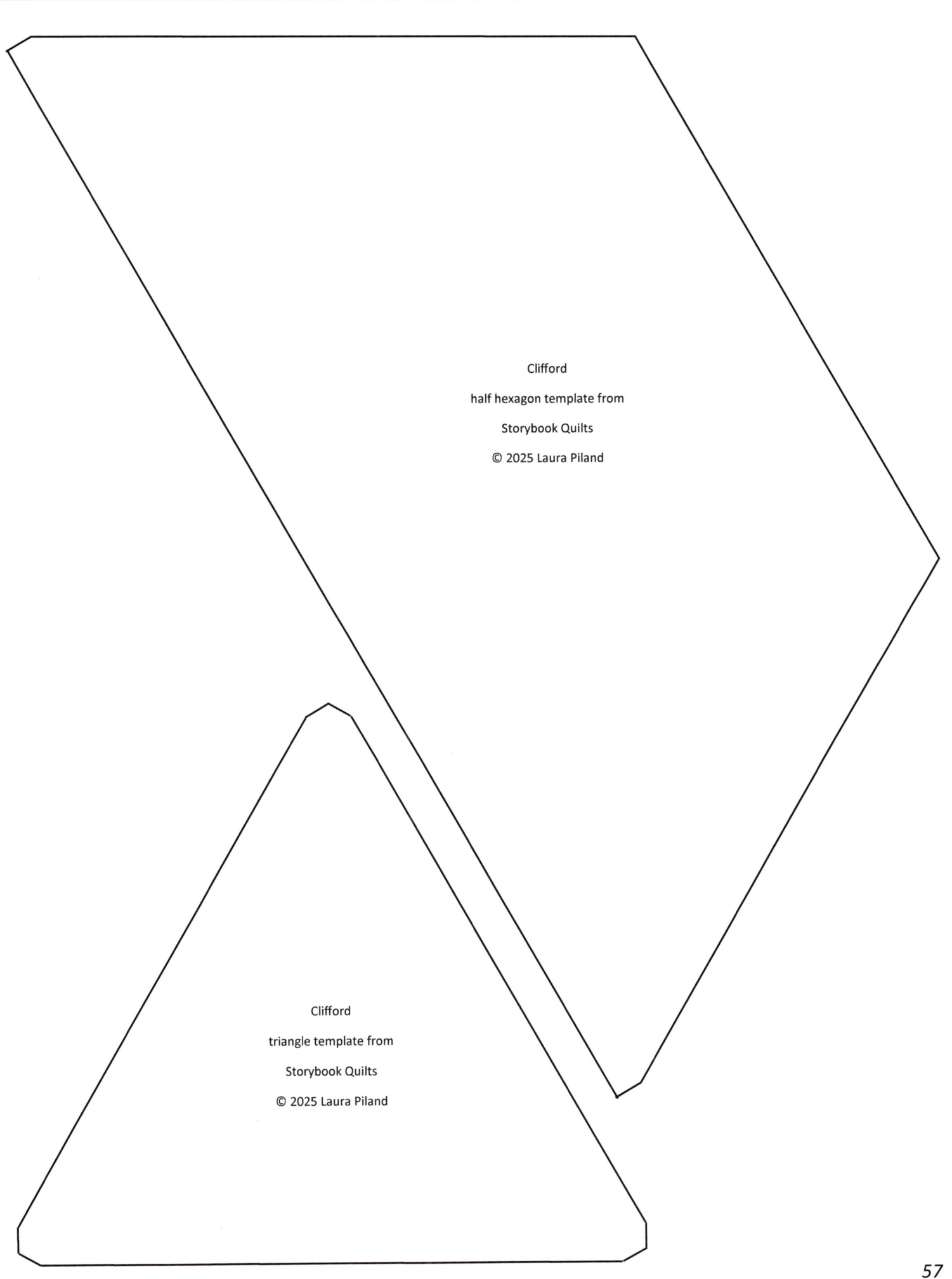

Clifford

half hexagon template from

Storybook Quilts

© 2025 Laura Piland

Clifford

triangle template from

Storybook Quilts

© 2025 Laura Piland

SEWING THE BLOCKS

Stitch a dark orange ¾" strip and a light orange 2 ⅜" strip together along one long side. A consistent ¼" seam is imperative, so take your time. Carefully press the seam toward the light orange fabric, make sure to press the strip in a straight line. Then sew another light orange 2 ⅜" strip to the other side of the dark orange strip. Carefully press this seam toward the light orange fabric. Repeat with all light orange and dark orange fabrics to make 6 strip sets.

Using the triangle template, trace a triangle onto the strip set, aligning one edge of the triangle with the bottom edge of the strip set. Then trace a second triangle next to and touching the first triangle, but align one triangle edge with the top edge of the strip set. Continue tracing the triangles in alternating directions to fill the strip set. Cut out the triangles with scissors or a rotary cutter. Repeat with all strip sets to make (72) triangle units.

Sew three triangle units together as shown to make a half hexagon. Press seams open. Repeat to make 24 half hexagon units.

ASSEMBLING THE QUILT TOP

Arrange the half hexagons into 17 rows with 9 half hexagons in each row. The diagram below shows the first row. Use the diagram on the next page as a guide, but the first and last hexagon in each row will be shaped like the image below. Be sure to place the print and pieced half hexagons facing the desired direction.

Sew the half hexagons together in each row. Press the seams in odd-numbered rows to the left; press the seams in even-numbered rows to the right.

Place rows 1 and 2 right sides together, carefully aligning the hexagons so like colors match up where needed. Pin the seam intersections. Sew the rows together. Press these long seams as desired. Repeat to sew all rows together. *(Note: Some rows will appear longer than others. Ignore that while sewing the rows together. Just focus on lining up the hexagons within each row with the previous row.)*

FINISHING THE QUILT

Once all the rows are sewn together, use a ruler and rotary cutter to trim off the left and right sides of the quilt. If you view the edge as mountains and valleys, then trim the edge even with the lowest valley.

Cut backing fabric into two equal lengths. Trim off selvages. Sew the two pieces together along the selvage edge using a ½" seam. Press this seam open.

Layer the backing fabric (right side down), batting, and quilt top (right side up) to make a quilt sandwich. Baste and quilt as desired.

For my version, I quilted horizontal straight lines about 1" apart. This could be done on a longarm or with a walking foot on a regular sewing machine. (I did it with my walking foot!)

Sew binding strips end to end, then bind the quilt using your favorite method. Make sure you add a label!

Goodnight Already *quilt*

In *Goodnight Already!*, written by Jory John and illustrated by Benji Davies, Bear is utterly exhausted and ready to drift off into a deep, peaceful sleep under his cozy quilt, but Bear's dreams are quickly interrupted by his neighbor, Duck, who is wide awake and bursting with energy. The result is a hilarious, relatable tale of mismatched energy, friendship boundaries, and the universal quest for a good night's sleep. With witty dialogue by Jory John and charming, expressive illustrations by Benji Davies, this bedtime story delights readers of all ages—especially those who know what it's like to be too tired...or too awake.

Visit www.sliceofpiquilts.com/StorybookQuilts to purchase the storybooks and quilt kits.

Quilt size: 36" x 42" (baby/lap)

MATERIALS

- Navy blue: 1 yard

- Medium blue: 1 ¼ yards

- ⅓ yard for binding

- 1 ½ yards for backing

- Fusible web like Lite Steam-A-Seam 2: 18" x 2 yards

- Crib-sized batting

CUTTING

Trace the template from page 63 onto template plastic (or make a copy of the template onto cardstock) and cut out. Trace the shape onto the back of the fusible web as close together as you can to make 168 orange peel shapes.

Press the fusible web to the wrong side of the navy fabric following the manufacturer's directions. Cut out all shapes with scissors or carefully with a rotary cutter.

From the binding fabric, cut:

(4) 2 ½" x 40" strips

Tip!

It can be challenging to find an exact match in fabric to the colors in a storybook illustration, so sometimes close is good enough! For this quilt, try Painter's Palette solids by PBS Fabrics in Artesian and Navy, or Moda Bella solids in Little Boy Blue and Midnight, or Kona solid fabrics in Water and Navy.

ASSEMBLING THE QUILT TOP

Use chalk, a disappearing ink pen, or an air erasable fabric pen to draw horizontal and vertical lines every 3" on the medium blue fabric. You need 13 lines across the width of the fabric, and 15 lines across the length of the fabric. I like to draw a center line first, then draw lines on either side of it.

Remove the paper backing from an orange peel shape and place it diagonally in one square.

Repeat for all orange peel shapes, alternating their direction in each square. Use the diagram below as a guide.

Once all the orange peels are placed, press. (Note: The ink of some disappearing ink and air erasable pens can become permanent when pressed. Be sure to read the directions for the specific pen you use and do a test before pressing. Often, you just need to wait for the ink to disappear before pressing.)

FINISHING THE QUILT

This quilt uses a quilt-as-you-go method that stitches down the applique and adds the quilting at the same time.

Layer the backing fabric (right side down), batting, and quilt top (right side up) to make a quilt sandwich. Baste as desired.

Starting at the orange peel in one corner, use a walking foot to stitch along the right side of the orange peel, about ⅛" from the edge of the shape. When you reach the bottom of the shape, continue stitching onto the next orange peel, stitching on the left side. Continue in this "S" path until you reach the last orange peel in that diagonal row. Then pivot, and stitch back on the other side of the same orange peels in that diagonal row.

Continue stitching each diagonal row until all the orange peels are stitched down.

Sew binding strips end to end, then bind the quilt using your favorite method. Don't forget to add a label!

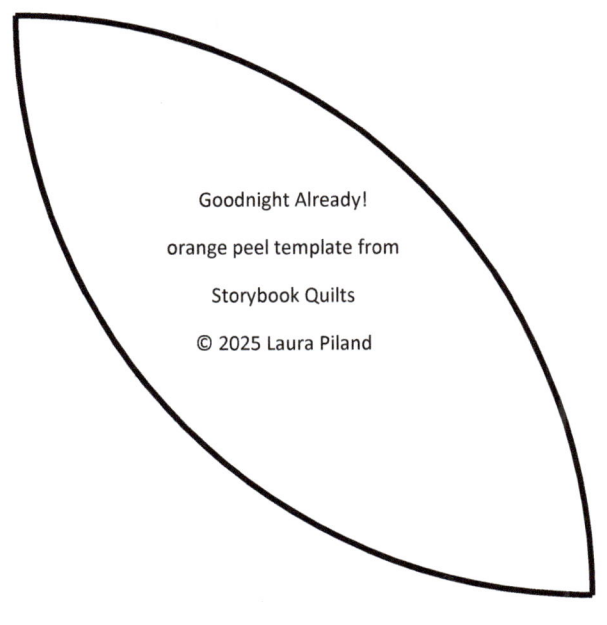

Goodnight Already!

orange peel template from

Storybook Quilts

© 2025 Laura Piland

Tip!

A walking foot (or even feed foot) is great for straight-line or gentle curve quilting. It helps feed the layers of the quilt evenly through the machine.

Make sure the walking foot arm rests on the needle clamp screw so the foot works properly. If the foot attaches to your machine with a screw, be sure to tighten it securely so it doesn't shift or vibrate loose during quilting.

Set your stitch length to about 3.5 for smoother quilting lines and less fabric distortion.

Slow and steady wins the race. It's called a walking foot for a reason!

Hello Lighthouse *quilt*

Hello Lighthouse by Sophie Blackall is a beautifully illustrated picture book that tells the story of a lighthouse keeper's life through the changing seasons. Dollhouse-like illustrations reveal his daily routines and the quiet rhythm of life by the sea as he tends the light, writes in his logbook, and waits for letters from his loved ones. Over time, he gets married and starts a family, and the lighthouse stands steadfast. The circle-themed quilt on the bed adds warmth and charm to the round home. The book is a poetic tribute to lighthouse keepers of the past, and to the enduring beauty of connection, change, and the sea.

Visit www.sliceofpiquilts.com/StorybookQuilts to purchase the storybooks and quilt kits.

Quilt size: 60" x 72" (throw)

MATERIALS

- Background: 3 ¾ yards
- Circle fabrics: (12) ⅓ yard cuts

(Note: If fussy cutting any of the fabrics, then more yardage will be required.)

- ½ yard for binding
- 4 yards for backing
- Twin-sized batting

(Note: Get the exact fabrics I used at the website listed above, or choose fabrics that are similar colors, or just use whatever fabrics you like for a scrappy look!)

Tip!

Would you rather have a larger bed-sized quilt or a smaller baby quilt? This storybook quilt is great for making in a different size just by making more or fewer blocks. Using 2 ¼ yards for the background and 12 fat quarters for the circle fabrics, you can make 16 blocks for a 48" x 48" baby quilt. Or you can make the quilt twin-sized by making 48 blocks with 6 yards of background fabric and ½ yard cuts for the circle fabrics.

CUTTING

From the background fabric, cut:

(30) 12 ½" x 12 ½" squares

(30) 3" x 3" squares

Trace the tumbler template from the next page onto template plastic (or make a photocopy of the template onto cardstock) and cut out. Trace the tumbler shape onto the circle fabrics then cut them out to make (30) from each fabric.

From the binding fabric, cut:

(7) 2 ½" x 40" strips

SEWING THE BLOCKS

Arrange 12 tumbler shapes (one from each circle fabric) into a circle shape. Sew the tumblers together in pairs as shown. Press the seams open.

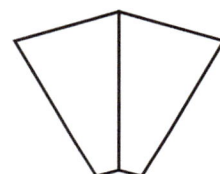

Sew the pairs together, joining all the tumblers to create a complete circle. Press seams open.

Repeat to make 30 circle units.

Trace the large circle template from the next page onto heat resistant template plastic (or make a photocopy of the template onto cardstock). Then line up the dotted line of the template with the one you just traced to trace it a second time, making one complete circle.

Lay a circle unit right side down on your ironing board, then center the large circle template on top. Carefully press the outside edges of the circle unit over the cardstock template. A metal stiletto may help, and you may like to paint or brush starch along the edge before pressing. Repeat for all circle units.

Trace the small circle template from the next page onto heat resistant template plastic (or make a photocopy of the template onto cardstock) and cut out. Lay the circle in the center of a 3" background square and cut around the circle about ¼" away from the template. Thread a needle and take small basting stitches in the seam allowance. Leave a thread tail on both ends. Place the template on the wrong side of the fabric circle and pull up on the thread tails to gather the seam allowance around the circle. Press the seam allowance in place. Pull out the circle template and knot the thread tails.

Repeat to make 30 small circles.

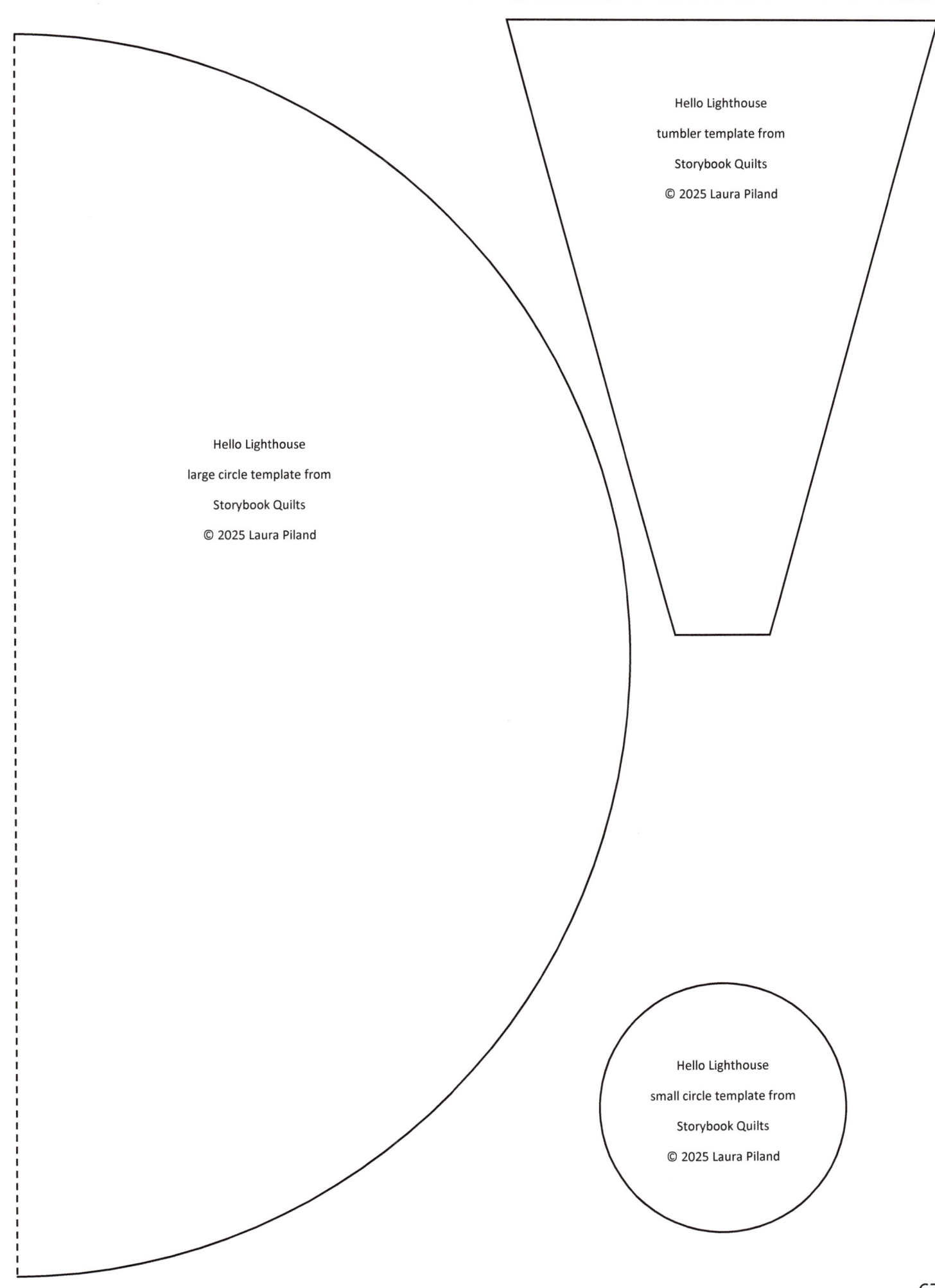

Hello Lighthouse
tumbler template from
Storybook Quilts
© 2025 Laura Piland

Hello Lighthouse
large circle template from
Storybook Quilts
© 2025 Laura Piland

Hello Lighthouse
small circle template from
Storybook Quilts
© 2025 Laura Piland

SEWING THE BLOCKS, CONTINUED

Fold a background square in half horizontally and lightly press. Repeat to create a light vertical crease too.

Center the circle unit on the background square, using the crease lines as a guide. Pin well or glue baste.

Place a small circle in the center of the block. Pin or glue baste.

Stitch around the edge of the circle unit and the small circle to secure them to the background fabric. I used a straight stitch about ⅛" away from the edge of the fabric. You could also use a zig zag or blanket stitch—or you could hand stitch them! As you sew, make sure the raw edge is tucked under to create a smooth circle edge.

Repeat for all 30 blocks.

ASSEMBLING THE QUILT TOP

Arrange the blocks into 6 rows with 5 blocks in each row. Be sure to place the blocks all facing the same direction. Use the diagram on the next page as a guide.

Sew the blocks together in each row. Press the seams in odd-numbered rows to the left; press the seams in even-numbered rows to the right.

Sew the rows together, nesting seams. Press these long seams down.

METHODS FOR MAKING CIRCLES

There are several methods of making circles for the centers of the blocks. Instead of hand stitching them, you could use freezer paper! For this, trace the small circle template onto the dull side of a piece of freezer paper (yes, the roll right from your kitchen!). Place this piece of freezer paper on top of a second piece (both shiny sides down). Press to adhere both papers together, then cut out the circle.

Press this freezer paper circle (shiny side down) to the wrong side of a 3" background square. Trim the background fabric about ¼" away from the circle.

Using a paintbrush or cotton swab, coat the edge of the fabric with starch. Press the fabric over the edge of the circle. A metal stiletto (or your seam ripper!) can be helpful. Ease in the fullness to make the edges smooth.

Peel off the freezer paper—then use it again for the next one! After making all the circles, glue or pin them to the centers of the blocks then stitch around the edge.

Or a third method: you could use raw-edge applique! Trace the small circle template onto fusible web, press that to the 3" background square, and cut out. Then just press the circle in the center of the blocks and machine stitch around the edge!

FINISHING THE QUILT

Cut backing fabric into two equal lengths. Trim off selvages. Sew the two pieces together along the selvage edge using a ½" seam. Press this seam open.

Layer the backing fabric (right side down), batting, and quilt top (right side up) to make a quilt sandwich. Baste and quilt as desired.

For my version, I used a medium-sized free-motion meander design to quilt the background. I chose not to quilt over the circles, but you could! You could free-motion quilt over them, custom quilt them, or use a walking foot to stitch in the ditch.

Sew binding strips end to end, then bind the quilt using your favorite method. Be sure to include a label on the quilt too!

Alexander and the Terrible, Horrible, No Good, Very Bad Day *quilt*

In *Alexander and the Terrible, Horrible, No Good, Very Bad Day* by Judith Viorst, a young boy named Alexander wakes up with gum in his hair, and things only get worse from there. His day spirals into a series of unfortunate events and disappointments. No matter where he goes or what he does, things continue to go wrong. Alexander says he wants to move to Australia, where he thinks things would be better. At the end of his very bad day, Alexander crawls into bed under his quilt, still feeling frustrated. But his mom reminds him that some days are just like that—even in Australia.

Visit www.sliceofpiquilts.com/StorybookQuilts to purchase the storybooks and quilt kits.

Quilt size: 55" x 65" (throw)

MATERIALS

- Purple: ¼ yard
- Pink: 1 ½ yards
- Blue: 1 yard
- White: ¼ yard
- Yellow: 1 yard
- Green: 1 yard

(Note: The colors of Kona solid fabric by Robert Kaufman that are close to what I used are Mulberry (purple), Pomegranate (pink), Hyacinth (blue), White, Citrus (yellow), and Peridot (green).)

- ½ yard for binding
- 3 ½ yards for backing
- Twin-sized batting

Tip!

Many different versions of this storybook have been printed over the years since it was originally published in 1987. Depending on the version you have, the quilt on the cover of the book may be colored differently. In some versions, the colors may match or be very similar to the ones I used. In others, the colors are completely different! Use the storybook illustration on your book as a guide in choosing the colors for your quilt.

CUTTING

From the purple fabric, cut:

(2) 1 ½" x WOF (width of fabric) strips, then subcut into:

      (50) 1 ½" squares

From the pink fabric, cut:

(6) 5 ½" x WOF strips, then subcut into:

      (4) 5 ½" x 40" strips

      (4) 5 ½" x 16" strips

(14) 1 ½" x WOF strips, then subcut into:

      (100) 1 ½" x 3 ½" rectangles

      (100) 1 ½" x 1 ½" squares

From the blue fabric, cut:

(25) 1 ½" x WOF strips, then subcut into:

      (100) 1 ½" x 5 ½" rectangles

      (100) 1 ½" x 3 ½" squares

From the white fabric, cut:

(3) 2 ¼" x WOF strips, then subcut into:

      (49) 2 ¼" x 2 ¼" squares, cut in half diagonally *once* to yield (98) A1 and B1 triangles

From the yellow fabric, cut:

(20) 1 ¾" x WOF strips, then subcut into:

      (98) 1 ¾" x 3 ½" (A2 and B2) rectangles

      (98) 1 ¾ x 4 ¼" (A3 and B3) rectangles

From the green fabric, cut:

(7) 4 ¾" x WOF strips, then subcut into:

      (49) 4 ¾" x 4 ¾" squares, cut in half diagonally *once* to yield (98) A4 and B4 triangles

From the binding fabric, cut:

(7) 2 ½" x 40" strips

SEWING THE BLOCKS

This quilt is made with two different quilt blocks. One is traditionally pieced, and one is paper pieced.

First, let's make the traditionally pieced square blocks.

Sew a pink 1 ½" square to the top and bottom of a purple 1 ½" square. Press seams toward the pink fabrics.

Stitch a pink 1 ½" x 3 ½" rectangle to the left and right sides of this unit. Press seams toward the pink fabrics.

Stitch a blue 1 ½" x 3 ½" rectangle to the top and bottom of the unit. Press seams toward the blue fabric.

Stitch a blue 1 ½" x 5 ½" rectangle to the left and right sides of the unit. Press seams toward the blue fabric.

Repeat to make 50 square blocks.

  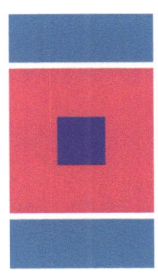  

Now let's make the paper-pieced blocks.

Trace or photocopy the templates from page 74. Using the white, yellow, and green pieces (labeled A1/B1, A2/B2, A3/B3, and A4/B4 during cutting), paper piece one A and one B unit. Stitch the A and B units together along the long edge to make one block. Carefully tear away the paper and press.

Repeat to make 49 blocks.

ASSEMBLING THE QUILT TOP

Use the diagram on page 75 as a guide and arrange the blocks into 11 rows with 9 blocks in each row. Be sure to alternate the blocks, but pay attention to the orientation of each block.

Sew the blocks together in each row. Press the seams in odd-numbered rows to the left; press the seams in even-numbered rows to the right.

Sew the rows together, nesting seams. Press these long seams as desired.

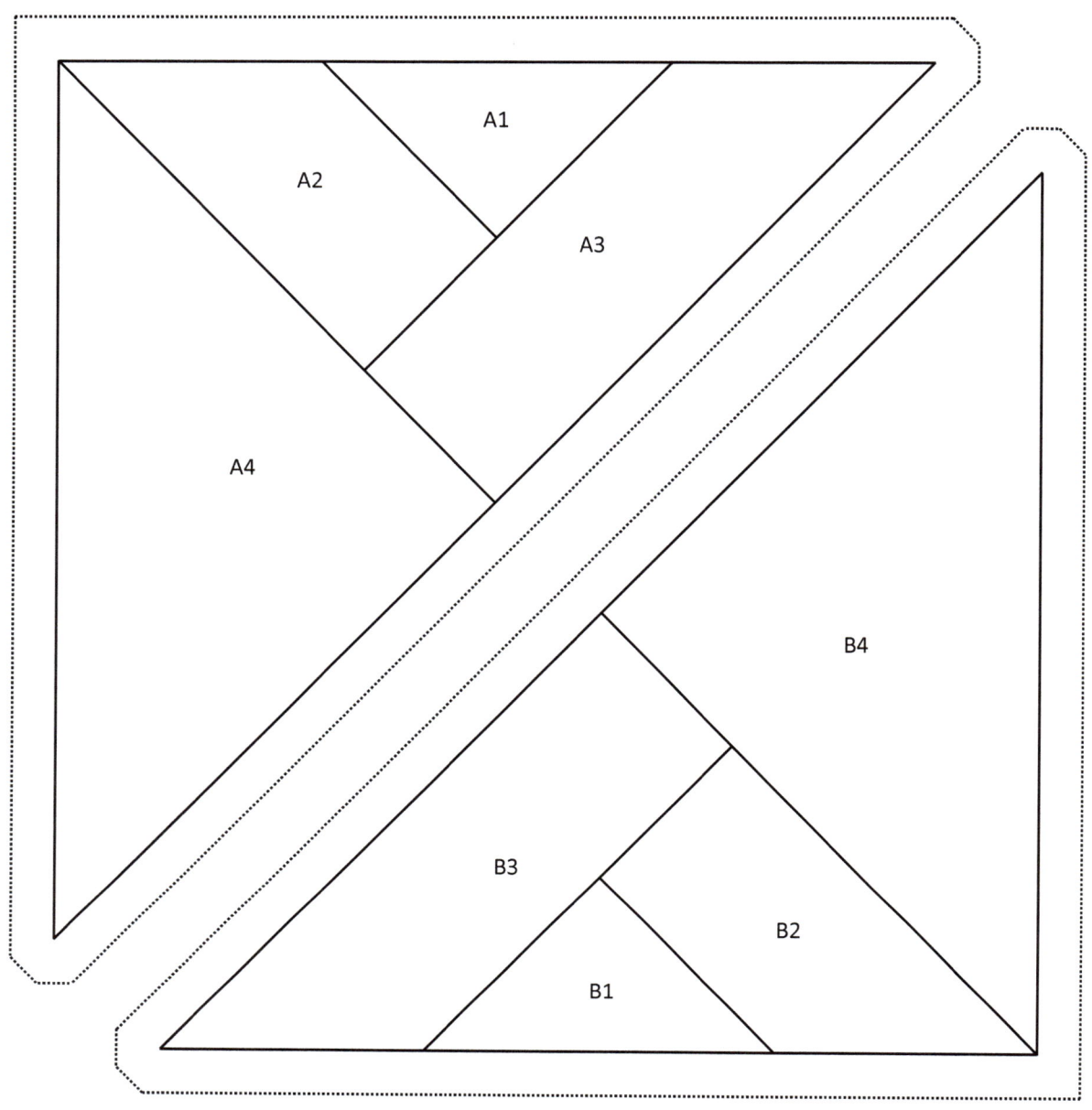

Alexander

Paper piecing template from

Storybook Quilts

© 2025 Laura Piland

PAPER PIECING WITH FREEZER PAPER

If you don't want to make 49 copies of this page to paper piece and then tear out the paper from the blocks after sewing, try freezer paper! Trace or photocopy this page onto freezer paper. Fold the template on all lines. Place the first two fabrics into position, but before sewing, fold the freezer paper back on that seam line, then stitch with your needle right next to the paper fold, but not through the paper. Press, then position the next fabric. Just before sewing, peel back the freezer paper and fold it on that seam line. Stitch right next to the fold, but not through the paper. Continue until unit A is finished, then peel the freezer paper off. Repeat for unit B. You can reuse the same freezer paper templates for all the blocks!

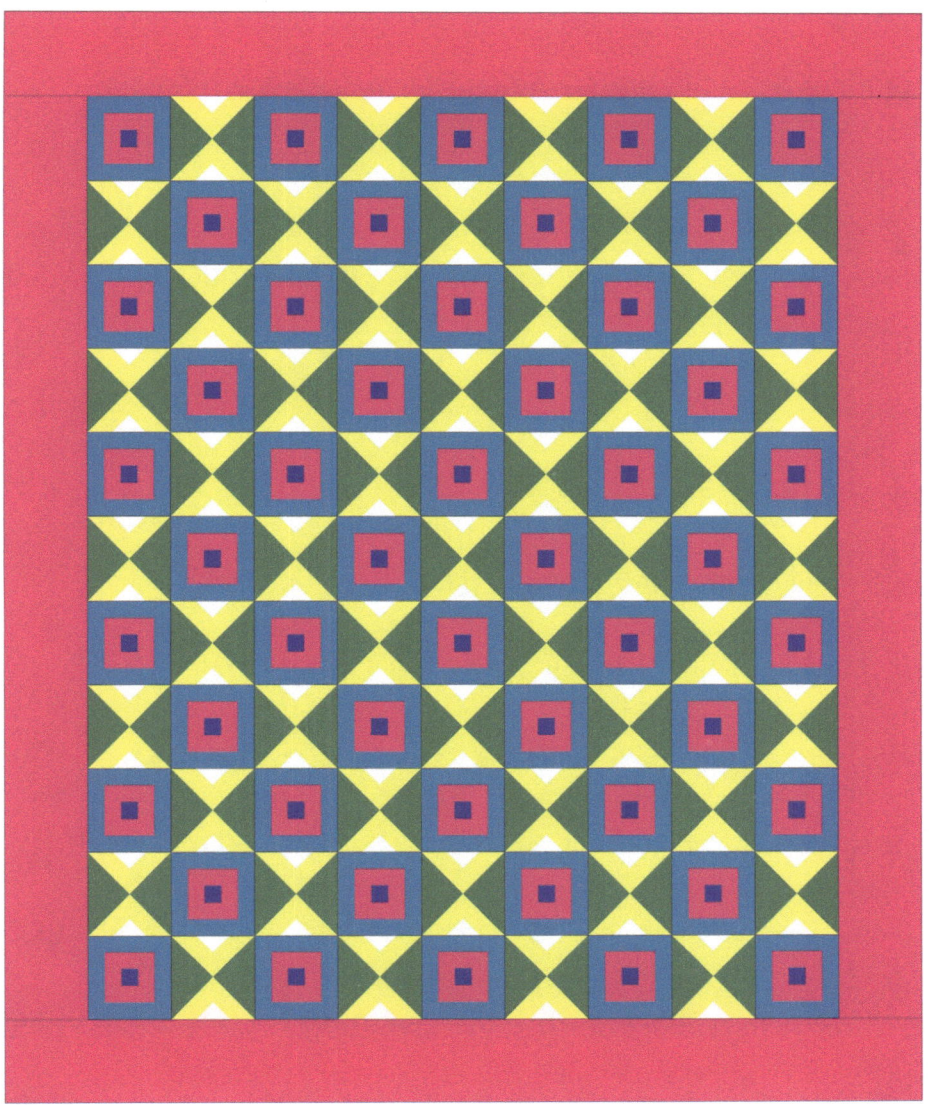

ADDING THE BORDERS

Sew a 5 ½" x 40" pink strip and a 5 ½" x 16" pink strip end to end. Press seam as desired. Repeat to make four border strips. (See the "tip" on page 33 for sewing borders to the quilt top.)

Sew a border strip to the left side of the quilt top. Press seam towards the border fabric. Repeat for the right side.

Sew a border strip to the top edge of the quilt top. Press seam towards the border fabric. Repeat for the bottom edge.

FINISHING THE QUILT

Layer the backing fabric (right side down), batting, and quilt top (right side up) to make a quilt sandwich. Baste and quilt as desired.

For my version, I used my walking foot to stitch in the ditch along the "X" seams of the paper-pieced blocks. (See page 15 for more information about stitching in the ditch.)

Sew binding strips end to end, then bind the quilt using your favorite method. Don't forget to add a label!

BIBLIOGRAPHY

Listed below are the 14 children's books that inspired the quilt patterns in this book.

Bardhan-Quallen, Sudipta. *Chicks Run Wild*. Illustrated by Ward Jenkins, Simon & Schuster Books for Young Readers, 2011. ISBN 978-1442406735.

Blackall, Sophie. *Hello Lighthouse*. Little, Brown Books for Young Readers, 2018. ISBN 978-0316362382.

Bridwell, Norman. *Clifford the Small Red Puppy*. Scholastic, 1972. ISBN 978-0590442947.

Cooney, Barbara. *Miss Rumphius*. Viking Press, 1982. ISBN 978-0670479580.

Dewdney, Anna. *Llama Llama Red Pajama*. Viking, 2005. ISBN 978-0451474575.

Doerrfeld, Cori. *Beneath*. Little, Brown Books for Young Readers, 2023. ISBN 978-0316312264.

Gehrisch, Becky. *Escape to Play*. Bookling Media, 2021.ISBN 978-1954376007.

Hughes-Odgers, Kyle. *Can a Skeleton Have an X-ray?* Fremantle Press, 2015. ISBN 978-1925162691.

John, Jory. *Goodnight Already!*. Illustrated by Benji Davies, HarperCollins, 2014. ISBN 978-0062286208.

Mayer, Mercer. *All by Myself*. Golden Press, 1983. ISBN 978-0307119384.

Oppenheim, Joanne. *The Prince's Bedtime*. Illustrated by Miriam Latimer, Barefoot Books, 2006. ISBN 978-1841485973.

Viorst, Judith. *Alexander and the Terrible, Horrible, No Good, Very Bad Day*. Atheneum Books for Young Readers, 1972. ISBN 978-0689711732.

Wahl, Phoebe. *Little Witch Hazel: A Year in the Forest*. Tundra Books, 2021. ISBN 978-0735264892.

Wilson, Karma. *Bear Can't Sleep*. Illustrated by Jane Chapman, Margaret K. McElderry Books, 2018. ISBN 978-1481459730.

RESOURCES

The quilts in this book are intentionally designed to echo the look and feel of the illustrations found in beloved children's picture books. Each pattern was created with careful attention to the visual details that make those storybook scenes so magical—including the color palettes and fabric shapes. In many cases, I didn't just design a quilt that matched the picture—I also created custom fabrics to make it possible for you to recreate the quilts too! These original fabrics were inspired by elements in the illustrations, allowing the finished quilts to feel like they've leapt right off the page. My goal was to make each quilt feel like an extension of the story, transforming the warmth of a good book into something tangible, memorable, and heartfelt. Whether displayed in a nursery, draped over a reading chair, or gifted to a young reader, these quilts are meant to bring stories to life in a new and creative way.

Purchase the fabric, panels, and kits at **www.sliceofpiquilts.com/StorybookQuilts**.

See my latest quilt finish and sign up for my newsletter at **https://www.sliceofpiquilts.com**.

Find me on social media as Slice of Pi Quilts or @sliceofpiquilts.

Join my community at **https://www.facebook.com/groups/quiltingandsewingdeals**.

Shop all of my quilt patterns and products in my shop: **https://sliceofpiquilts.etsy.com**.

Know a child that would like to learn to quilt? Find kits, lessons, and more at **https://myveryfirstquilt.com**.

YOU MAY ALSO LIKE

I designed my first quilt pattern in 2016, and have since released over 30 more! My patterns are fun, creative, and easy to follow. If you're making a special gift or wanting to try something new, check out all of the Slice of Pi Quilts patterns in my shop: **https://sliceofpiquilts.etsy.com**.

MY VERY FIRST QUILT

Engage your child's creative side through the timeless art of quilting! Experience the convenience of virtual lessons coupled with the assurance of a carefully curated materials kit delivered directly to your doorstep. Not only will your child learn a traditional craft, but they'll also develop patience, fine motor skills, and confidence! Invest in your child's future and encourage them to make their very first quilt!

- Choose your kit - Pick your favorite color or fabric, and we'll ship it to you!

- Watch the videos - Six videos take you from threading the sewing machine to finishing the quilt!

- Make a quilt! - Sew along with the videos to make your very own quilt!

Find beginner pillowcase and quilt kits at **https://myveryfirstquilt.com**.

ABOUT THE AUTHOR

Laura Piland is the creative force behind *Slice of Pi Quilts* and the designer of the popular Exploding Heart quilt pattern. Her quilting journey began in 2010 when she made a quilt for a friend's baby—a project that sparked an unexpected and enduring passion. Since then, Laura has made over 500 quilts, each one reflecting her love for the craft and her commitment to making quilting fun, approachable, and inspiring.

A former math teacher and now a homeschooling mom of three boys, Laura brings a unique blend of structure and creativity to her designs. Her quilting style is eclectic, spanning modern to traditional, and she rarely makes the same quilt twice. Laura thrives on experimenting with new techniques and ideas, constantly challenging the "quilt police."

In 2016, she started *Slice of Pi Quilts* to share her original patterns and connect with the quilting community. Since then, she has taught workshops at quilt shops and guilds across the country and founded the popular Quilting & Sewing Deals Facebook group, helping quilters discover tools, notions, and supplies at the best prices.

In 2023, Laura launched *My Very First Quilt*, an online program designed to teach kids how to make their very first quilt. Fueled by her passion for education and creativity, the program empowers children to build confidence, develop new skills, and experience the joy of creating something meaningful with their own hands.

Through *Storybook Quilts*, Laura invites quilters of all ages to bring their favorite stories to life with fabric. Each pattern in the book is designed to ignite imagination, celebrate storytelling, and turn the quilting process into a creative journey as rich as the books that sparked it.

www.sliceofpiquilts.com

www.myveryfirstquilt.com